YEARNING FOR YOU, MY GOD

for Pat,
with appreciation,
Jim

YEARNING FOR YOU, MY GOD

A companion for praying

the Psalms

JAMES TORRENS, SJ

ART BY FR. JOHN GRIESBACH

TWENTY-THIRD PUBLICATIONS

TWENTY-THIRD PUBLICATIONS
1 Montauk Avenue, Suite 200, New London, CT 06320
(860) 437-3012 » (800) 321-0411 » www.twentythirdpublications.com

ISBN: 978-1-62785-217-3
Library of Congress Catalog Card Number: 2016909033
Printed in the U.S.A.

 A Division of Bayard, Inc.

CONTENTS

ART

PREFACE

How strange that the psalter, that anthology of very Jewish praises and supplications whose music we have lost, has come to be a centerpiece of Christian prayer. Often the psalms seem obsessed with the menace of enemies and eager to even the score. This seems to put them way out of tune with what Jesus urges in the Sermon on the Mount. Why do we hold the psalms so dear?

We know something of the history. The Desert Fathers, back in the early church, adopted this compilation of inspired prayers for continual recitation. It was ready-made for their solitude. The monastic orders in Europe took their lead, Benedictines above all, and the Liturgy of the Hours gradually emerged. The Divine Office became normative for priests and many religious, and a staple for lay piety as well.

My familiarity with the psalms goes back to the pocket edition I carried as a teenager. The seminary later imbued me with them in Latin. At this late date I have a handful of my favorites by memory, plus assorted verses or passages that have simply adhered to me, like lines of Shakespeare. So the time seems ripe for me to share my fondness for them, with brief meditations on a pick of my favorites, sampling the various types. I offer this collection as a help, even a spur, to familiarity with the psalms and affection for them.

Where does the millennial appeal of the psalms really lie? As prayers they engage us by their intensity and emotional force. "Pour out your hearts before [God]," they say (Psalm 62). We sense a real voice, often a communal one, pleading or arguing with the divine, or just breathlessly admiring. We are taken by their rhythmical eloquence. God, the addressee, is always their magnetic center. What the psalms offer most compellingly is encouragement to trust God, whatever the obstacles or enemies standing between us. Confidence in God's care, as Erik Erikson claimed, is the touchstone of the religious spirit.

Monsignor John Griesbach, Director of Saint Anthony Retreat at Three Rivers, California, joins me in this project. His contemplative paintings, inspired by the foothills of the Sierra Nevada, make the visual aspect of many psalms come alive. He illuminates the visible work of the Creator, as do so many of these deathless Palestinian texts.

My principal sources have been the *New Collegeville Bible Commentary* by Dianne Bergant, in two volumes, and the two volumes by Richard J. Clifford in the *Abingdon Old Testament Commentaries*. I have resorted, of course, to *The Jerome Biblical Commentary* and *The International Bible Commentary*. I am indebted to Leopold Sabourin, SJ, *The Psalms, their Origin and Meaning*, and to Robert Alter's classic, *The Art of Biblical Poetry*.

ARTIST'S WORD

The paintings that accompany the psalms in this volume are the fruit of my passion for landscape art. I can only hope that they produce in others the delight that I myself have had in executing them.

My calling to such art began in my family's sawmill and lumber yard in Tulare, California. We had stacks of lumber drying there in the sun, facing east toward the huge wall of the Sierra Nevada, about twenty miles distant. In the springtime, after snows, the Sierra has a cloak of white. I would climb up on the lumber stacks and sit for hours gazing there, lost in the beauty and wonder of it.

I owe my concentration on art to the end of my competing in sports. When I threw out my hip pitching softball, I needed another passion. It was then that an interest in oil painting bubbled up. I was director of vocations for the Fresno diocese, and my secretary, herself a teacher of art, steered me to a master teacher, Gary Langdon. For ten years, on my weekly day off, I attended his classes, where he taught me to work through the problems that would come up with each new canvas.

My landscape art coincides with my Ignatian form of prayer, finding God in all things. Painting for me has been a form of meditation. Contemplation of nature is the climate of my interior life, and the psalms are right at home there. They are songs that the human heart is singing about all the different ways we are in relationship to God and to ourselves and others. My paintings, I have often felt, are like songs that I sing; but instead of notes, I write out images.

There is always something more going on in my paintings for me than what you see on the surface. I came to realize that they were about giving voice to some of the deeper dimensions of my life and heart, which translate out in this visual way. A man complimented me once for the outstretched arms I had put into the scene of a Sierra lake. I had intended no such thing; but looking closely at certain shapes in it, I had to admit he was right.

No wonder that when I paint I have great peace and lose all sense of time. The right brain takes over, the one responsible for spatial relationships rather than language. In my alternate language of art, I hope to share the expressiveness of the psalms, and so echo their divine praises.

IN FAVOR

OF PSALMS

Though all Scripture is fragrant with God's grace, the Book of Psalms has a special attractiveness.

In the Book of Psalms there is profit for all, with healing power for our salvation. There is instruction from history, teaching from the law, prediction from prophecy, chastisement from denunciation, persuasion from moral preaching. All who read it may find the cure for their own individual failings. All with eyes to see can discover a complete gymnasium for the soul, a stadium for all the virtues, equipped for every kind of exercise; it is for each to choose the kind that is judged best to help gain the prize.

What no one would have dared to say was foretold by the psalmist alone, and afterward proclaimed by the Lord himself in the gospel.

FROM THE *Explanations of the Psalms*
BY ST. AMBROSE, BISHOP

Psalm 1

The Hebrew psalter begins with a sharp distinction between the two ways, one responsive to the law of God, the other not. No wonder Christianity was at first called the Way. Psalm 1 marks out the black and white of faithfulness to the commandments.

Since the entire Book of Psalms, the *Tehillim*, starts off with a beatitude—"Happy the one…"—small wonder that Matthew in his gospel has Jesus do the same for the Sermon on the Mount. Jesus was consciously fulfilling the Scriptures.

For an image of true holiness, Psalm 1 has us envision well-watered growth, the flourishing of trees near streams. In the American West, cottonwood trees fulfill this role, indicative of water. Their rootless opposite is tumbleweed.

*Lord, help me to find
the way, your way.*

Happy are those
who do not follow the advice of the wicked,
or take the path that sinners tread,
or sit in the seat of scoffers;
but their delight is in the law of the Lord,
and on his law they meditate day and night.
They are like trees
planted by streams of water,
which yield their fruit in its season,
and their leaves do not wither.
In all that they do, they prosper.
The wicked are not so,
but are like chaff that the wind drives away.
Therefore the wicked will not stand in the judgment,
nor sinners in the congregation of the righteous;
for the Lord watches over the way of the righteous,
but the way of the wicked will perish.

Psalm 8

Psalm 8 is a hymn in tune with the opening of Genesis. It puts itself in the place of anyone who has loved to sit out under the stars, as Saint Ignatius Loyola did in Rome, and find the Creator's hand in them: "O LORD, our Sovereign, how majestic is your name through all the earth!"

We do not need the Hubbell telescope to recognize how infinitesimal we are and to wonder how God could even notice us, not to say favor us. Yet we are given rule over God's works, with all else being put under our feet.

The abuse of our earthly environment and our prodigal way with its resources have been at times blamed on this Scripture. Judeo-Christians have been called insensitive masters. If so, shame on us, for the "rule" we are given is charged with responsibility.

Psalm 8 concludes as it began, with awe at the beauty around us, whose stewards we are.

Help me tend the world
you have made so dear.

PSALM 8

O Lord, our Sovereign,
how majestic is your name in all the earth!
You have set your glory above the heavens.
Out of the mouths of babes and infants
you have founded a bulwark because of your foes,
to silence the enemy and the avenger.
When I look at your heavens, the work of your fingers,
the moon and the stars that you have established;
what are human beings that you are mindful of them,
mortals that you care for them?
Yet you have made them a little lower than God,
and crowned them with glory and honor.
You have given them dominion over the works of your hands;
you have put all things under their feet,
all sheep and oxen,
and also the beasts of the field,
the birds of the air, and the fish of the sea,
whatever passes along the paths of the seas.
O Lord, our Sovereign,
how majestic is your name in all the earth!

Psalm 16

In the Liturgy of the Hours, Psalm 16 appears for recitation on Thursday at Night Prayer. That is just right for its attitude of resting tranquilly in God.

"Lord, my allotted portion and my cup, / you have made my destiny secure." Receiving minor orders in the seminary, which committed me to the celibate state, I heard the bishop recite these words over me in Latin. I have felt the impulse, and the need, to repeat them often.

Psalm 16 affirms the Lord God to be at the power position at one's right hand. This awareness buoys one up fully. Such a good Master will never let me fall into dark oblivion—the Pit. No wonder St. Peter, in his Pentecost sermon, could apply this psalm to the resurrection of Jesus.

The psalms as a whole are reticent about a future life. Psalm 16 is perhaps the most assertive about the "fullness of joy" in store.

Lord, my precious heritage,
lead me into your joy.

Protect me, O God, for in you I take refuge.
I say to the LORD, "You are my Lord;
I have no good apart from you."
As for the holy ones in the land, they are the noble,
in whom is all my delight.
Those who choose another god multiply their sorrows;
their drink offerings of blood I will not pour out
or take their names upon my lips.
The LORD is my chosen portion and my cup;
you hold my lot.
The boundary lines have fallen for me in pleasant places;
I have a goodly heritage.
I bless the LORD who gives me counsel;
in the night also my heart instructs me.
I keep the LORD always before me;
because he is at my right hand, I shall not be moved.
Therefore my heart is glad, and my soul rejoices;
my body also rests secure.
For you do not give me up to Sheol,
or let your faithful one see the Pit.
You show me the path of life.
In your presence there is fullness of joy;
in your right hand are pleasures forevermore.

Psalm 19

Psalm 19 has two very distinct parts; we meditate here on the first half of it. Remarkably, these verses, with their skyward gaze, make the sun into an apostle. The sun's display is meant to enlighten its admirers. (The panoply of stars does the same by night.) No one on earth can miss this message about the glory of God. St. Francis of Assisi put it memorably in "The Canticle of the Sun."

We know that, in our time, not all astronomers are theists. They are bent on asking what, not who, set off the Big Bang. In 1870, Vatican Council I presented a brief for the existence of God, reasserting that human wisdom unaided should be aware of the Creator, and can be a handmaid of faith.

St. Augustine, surveying the wonders of earth, sea, and sky, put this question: "Who made these beautiful changing things?" Who indeed, he answered, "if not one who is beautiful and changes not." So says Psalm 19.

> *How can I stay deaf*
> *while the heavens proclaim?!*

PSALM 19:1-6

The heavens are telling the glory of God;
and the firmament proclaims his handiwork.
Day to day pours forth speech,
and night to night declares knowledge.
There is no speech, nor are there words;
their voice is not heard;
yet their voice goes out through all the earth,
and their words to the end of the world.
In the heavens he has set a tent for the sun,
which comes out like a bridegroom from his wedding canopy,
and like a strong man runs its course with joy.
Its rising is from the end of the heavens,
and its circuit to the end of them;
and nothing is hid from its heat.

You visit the earth and water it, you greatly enrich it;

the river of God is full of water;

you provide the people with grain,

for so you have prepared it.

You water its furrows abundantly,

settling its ridges,

softening it with showers,

and blessing its growth.

You crown the year with your bounty;

your wagon tracks overflow with richness.

The pastures of the wilderness overflow,

the hills gird themselves with joy.

Psalm 65:9–12

Psalm 22

How painful it is to intone this psalm, knowing that Jesus himself did so as a last word upon the cross. Saint Matthew found the death of Jesus to be inscribed in these verses, prophetic in phrasing and imagery. He drew upon them heavily to frame his account of our Lord's passion.

Psalm 22, an individual lament, hits home for any who find themselves desperate before God. These opening verses of the psalm are spoken by someone seeing himself as "a worm, and not human, / scorned by others." He vividly imagines himself the prey of vicious animals and parched by an extremity of thirst ("my tongue sticks to my jaws"), as is every victim of crucifixion.

From the start, the psalmist remembers God as having come dramatically to the rescue of the people. Why so mute and distant now? What urgency there is to the plea that closes our segment, and the next one as well: "Be not far from me."

Dear Savior on your cross,
be not far from me.

My God, my God, why have you forsaken me?
Why are you so far from helping me,
from the words of my groaning?
O my God, I cry by day, but you do not answer;
and by night, but find no rest.
Yet you are holy,
enthroned on the praises of Israel.
In you our ancestors trusted;
they trusted, and you delivered them.
To you they cried, and were saved;
in you they trusted, and were not put to shame.
But I am a worm, and not human;
scorned by others, and despised by the people.
All who see me mock at me;
they make mouths at me, they shake their heads;
"Commit your cause to the LORD; let him deliver—
let him rescue the one in whom he delights!"
Yet it was you who took me from the womb;
you kept me safe on my mother's breast.
On you I was cast from my birth,
and since my mother bore me you have been my God.
Do not be far from me,
for trouble is near
and there is no one to help.

Psalm 23

Is any text of the Hebrew Testament more familiar than the Good Shepherd psalm? Psalm 23 is about trusting in divine rule and care in that form specific to a pastoral people: shepherding. The details are so effective: green pasture, fresh water, the shepherd's staff with its crook, safe conduct through the hazards of "the darkest valley." Some translations have "the valley of the shadow of death." No wonder a funeral is unthinkable without some recitation or singing of the Good Shepherd psalm.

One intriguing thing about this psalm is its mixed metaphor, which writers are supposed to avoid. The Shepherd of a wool-bearing flock all of a sudden becomes the gracious Host. We can imagine Abraham spreading a succulent table for his three angelic guests. The Enemy, who is never far from Jewish anxieties, has to just sit and watch the banquet and stew with jealousy.

The two parts of Psalm 23 fit perfectly. The elegant banquet is a perfect end to the hazardous shepherding.

Good Shepherd, receive me
at your table, please.

PSALM 23

The LORD is my shepherd, I shall not want.
He makes me lie down in green pastures;
he leads me beside still waters;
he restores my soul.
He leads me in right paths
for his name's sake.
Even though I walk through the darkest valley,
I fear no evil;
for you are with me;
your rod and your staff—
they comfort me.
You prepare a table before me
in the presence of my enemies;
you anoint my head with oil;
my cup overflows.
Surely goodness and mercy shall follow me
all the days of my life,
and I shall dwell in the house of the LORD
my whole life long.

Psalm 27

This section of Psalm 27 reverberates with the awe that the Jews felt for their Temple, house of the Lord on earth, in whose loveliness God may be worshiped.

The Temple, for its part, has a forerunner in sacred history, the tent of witness, the Dwelling in the desert. The glory of God would at times fill the tent, or go before it, urging on the people of God. The speaker looks forward to receiving cover in God's tent.

The lines further on express a deep longing for God as our true resting place, despite dryness in prayer or heavy burdens. "Your face, Lord, do I seek. / Do not hide your face from me." These verses, trembling and insecure as they are, sum up all human desire for beatific vision, the Holy Face, *le beau Dieu.*

> *May my prayer be alive*
> *with urgent seeking.*

PSALM 27:4–9A

One thing I asked of the LORD,
that will I seek after:
to live in the house of the LORD
all the days of my life,
to behold the beauty of the LORD,
and to inquire in his temple.
For he will hide me in his shelter
in the day of trouble;
he will conceal me under the cover of his tent;
he will set me high on a rock.
Now my head is lifted up
above my enemies all around me,
and I will offer in his tent
sacrifices with shouts of joy;
I will sing and make melody to the LORD.
Hear, O LORD, when I cry aloud,
be gracious to me and answer me!
"Come," my heart says, "seek his face!"
Your face, LORD, do I seek.
Do not hide your face from me.
Do not turn your servant away in anger.

Psalm 33

The psalms are poetry for singing, probably a kind of chant. Even without a knowledge of Hebrew, we cannot fail to register the structural regularity of each psalm. Scholars call it a sense rhythm. The psalmist expresses some unit of meaning or of story, which he immediately rephrases or develops in a second line.

Psalm 33 is a hymn of praise put in the mouth of the community. Reading aloud this portion, one quickly gets into the swing. "By the word of the LORD the heavens were made," and then "all their hosts by the breath of his mouth."

Frequently the psalms are read or chanted as part of the Divine Office by two groups, sometimes in facing rows. This larger alternating rhythm, often sung in Gregorian chant without accompaniment, has served over the centuries to anchor the psalms firmly in Christian piety.

Over and over let me praise your work,
Creator Lord.

By the word of the LORD the heavens were made,
and all their host by the breath of his mouth.
He gathered the waters of the sea as in a bottle;
he put the deeps in storehouses.
Let all the earth fear the LORD;
let all the inhabitants of the world stand in awe of him.
For he spoke, and it came to be;
he commanded, and it stood firm.
The LORD brings the counsel of the nations to nothing;
he frustrates the plans of the peoples.
The counsel of the LORD stands forever,
the thoughts of his heart to all generations.
Happy is the nation whose God is the LORD,
the people whom he has chosen as his heritage.
The LORD looks down from heaven;
he sees all humankind.
From where he sits enthroned he watches
all the inhabitants of the earth—
he who fashions the hearts of them all,
and observes all their deeds.

For the LORD
is a great God,

and a great King
   above all gods.
In his hand are the depths
   of the earth;
the heights of the mountains
   are his also.

Psalm 95:3–4

Psalm 40

(vv. 6–10)

This early segment of Psalm 40 begins, "Sacrifice and offering you do not desire;…Then I said, 'Here I am; / in the scroll of the book it is written of me.'" The "scroll," according to Richard Clifford, is an immutable decree from on high. This passage says that observing God's will takes priority over ritual.

"Sacrifice and offering you do not desire…I delight to do your will," the psalmist says, echoing what Samuel told King Saul, "Obedience is better than sacrifice." This psalm is applied to Jesus the Messiah, whose obedience to the divine will brought a salvation that ritual sacrifice could not.

We have here a cluster of terms essential to Bible spirituality. In the "great congregation," the *cajal*, the psalmist will proclaim God's "deliverance" or *sedek* (often translated as "justice"), and will speak of God's "faithfulness," God's *emet*. *Emet* is about staying true, rock solid. "I have concealed your steadfast love," your *hesed*, the speaker says, referring to God's covenant love.

Here is my heart, on the altar
of your holy will.

Sacrifice and offering you do not desire,
but you have given me an open ear.
Burnt offering and sin offering
you have not required.
Then I said, "Here I am;
in the scroll of the book it is written of me.
I delight to do your will, O my God;
your law is within my heart."
I have told the glad news of deliverance
in the great congregation;
see, I have not restrained my lips,
as you know, O Lord.
I have not hidden your saving help within my heart,
I have spoken of your faithfulness and your salvation;
I have not concealed your steadfast love
and your faithfulness
from the great congregation.

Psalm 42

(vv. 1–7)

I was once in a car driving between a river and the woods when we hit a deer darting across for water. The opening of this psalm came quickly to mind: "As a deer longs for flowing streams, / so my soul longs for you, O God." The speaker is really yearning for the house of God in Jerusalem, but the words touch upon the inborn longing we have for God, for refreshment by the Holy Spirit.

The psalmist finds himself taunted by enemies about God's apparent distance: "Where is your God?" The adversaries are mostly exterior, but we can pray these words with a focus on our own interior foes.

In a compensatory mood, the psalmist floods with memories of ecstatic ritual at the house of God. What follows is a self-chiding for forgetfulness: "Why are you cast down, O my soul, and why are you disquieted within me? Hope in God." Do not let desolation sway you; consolation will return.

In a dry time, help me cherish
the graces past.

PSALM 42:1–7

As a deer longs for flowing streams,
so my soul longs for you, O God.
My soul thirsts for God,
for the living God.
When shall I come and behold the face of God?
My tears have been my food day and night,
while people say to me continually,
"Where is your God?"
These things I remember,
as I pour out my soul:
how I went with the throng,
and led them in procession to the house of God,
with glad shouts and songs of thanksgiving,
a multitude keeping festival.
Why are you cast down, O my soul,
and why are you disquieted within me?
Hope in God; for I shall again praise him,
my help and my God.
My soul is cast down within me;
therefore I remember you
from the land of Jordan and of Hermon,
from Mount Mizar.
Deep calls to deep
at the thunder of your cataracts;
all your waves and your billows
have gone over me.

Psalm 46

Psalm 46 has a message-bearing refrain, as do many of the psalms: "The LORD of hosts is with us; / The God of Jacob is our refuge." As someone who lives in earthquake country, susceptible to the Big One, I much need the boldness of those lines, and also these: "We will not fear, though the earth should change, / though the mountains shake in the heart of the sea."

For a refuge, the psalm puts us in the city of God, Sion, "the holy habitation of the Most High." Enemies may arrive in number to besiege the holy city with their battering, but it will hold.

The psalmist, finally, invites us to come see how God "breaks the bow and shatters the spear," and "burns the shields with fire," enforcing peace. Might we witness this more often! In a commanding voice, the Lord God speaks to our fearfulness, "Be still, and know that I am God!"

Be still, my soul.
Remember, the Lord is God.

God is our refuge and strength,
a very present help in trouble.
Therefore we will not fear, though the earth should change,
though the mountains shake in the heart of the sea;
though its waters roar and foam,
though the mountains tremble with its tumult.
There is a river whose streams make glad the city of God,
the holy habitation of the Most High.
God is in the midst of the city; it shall not be moved;
God will help it when the morning dawns.
The nations are in an uproar, the kingdoms totter;
he utters his voice, the earth melts.
The LORD of hosts is with us;
the God of Jacob is our refuge.
Come, behold the works of the LORD;
see what desolations he has brought on the earth.
He makes wars cease to the end of the earth;
he breaks the bow, and shatters the spear;
he burns the shields with fire.
"Be still, and know that I am God!
I am exalted among the nations,
I am exalted in the earth."
The LORD of hosts is with us;
the God of Jacob is our refuge.

Psalm 47

The psalms, often composed for cult in the Temple, were shaped in accord with certain literary types. Psalm 47 figures among those classified as Enthronement Psalms of Yahweh, that is, music bringing the assembly to God for veneration on the rightful throne.

Psalm 47 bursts into cheering for God at the very start. God is the Creator and Sustainer, to be revered worldwide by all nations, for he is in charge of all, but of Israel in particular, with a special providence.

The liturgy of the Ascension of Christ draws its motif, its refrain, from Psalm 47: "God has gone up with a shout; the Lord with the sound of a trumpet." The resurrected Jesus, we affirm, was taken up in view of the apostles to the enthronement of his humanity by the parent God, the "great king."

What excitement!
Our humanity is enthroned.

Clap your hands, all you peoples;
shout to God with loud songs of joy.
For the LORD, the Most High, is awesome,
a great king over all the earth.
He subdued peoples under us,
and nations under our feet.
He chose our heritage for us,
the pride of Jacob whom he loves.
God has gone up with a shout,
the LORD with the sound of a trumpet.
Sing praises to God, sing praises;
sing praises to our King, sing praises.
For God is the king of all the earth;
sing praises with a psalm.
God is king over the nations;
God sits on his holy throne.
The princes of the peoples gather
as the people of the God of Abraham.
For the shields of the earth belong to God;
he is highly exalted.

God alone is my rock and my salvation,

my fortress;

   I shall not be shaken.

On God rests my deliverance

and my honor,

my mighty rock;

my refuge is in God.

Psalm 62:6–7

Psalm 51

(vv. 1–10)

Psalm 51, known in the church by its opening word in Latin, *Miserere*, "Have mercy," is the chief of the penitential psalms. It is a litany of supplication for pardon and renewal of spirit. It is put in the mouth of King David because of his adultery with Bathsheba and the murder of her husband, Uriah. Psalm 51 would fit Saint Peter perfectly too, after his denial of knowing Christ. Thus the psalm applies both to synagogue and church.

"My sin is ever before me." Not that we should be haunted by guilt after receiving forgiveness, or keep confessing the past, but we need to stay aware of a humbling truth: "Indeed I was born guilty, / a sinner when my mother conceived me." This verse, an extreme of self-accusation, is a poetic figure born of compunction.

How many come to confession with longing for a clean heart! Surprisingly, an Easter spirit infuses the text, an assurance of gladness and joy.

> *Be merciful, dear risen Lord,*
> *to this sinner.*

Have mercy on me, O God,
according to your steadfast love;
according to your abundant mercy
blot out my transgressions.
Wash me thoroughly from my iniquity,
and cleanse me from my sin.
For I know my transgressions,
and my sin is ever before me.
Against you, you alone, have I sinned,
and done what is evil in your sight,
so that you are justified in your sentence
and blameless when you pass judgment.
Indeed, I was born guilty,
a sinner when my mother conceived me.
You desire truth in the inward being;
therefore teach me wisdom in my secret heart.
Purge me with hyssop, and I shall be clean;
wash me, and I shall be whiter than snow.
Let me hear joy and gladness;
let the bones that you have crushed rejoice.
Hide your face from my sins,
and blot out all my iniquities.
Create in me a clean heart, O God,
and put a new and right spirit within me.

Psalm 56

(vv. 1–11a)

Something keeps vexing me in the psalms: a preoccupation with enemies. It dominates the psalms numbered from 52 to 60, mostly called "laments."

Who are these enemies? Some are the Gentile oppressors of Israel, referred to as "the nations," who kept subjugating the Holy Land. Others seem much closer to home, conducting intrigues against the psalmist, laying traps, assaulting. They are like lions (Psalm 17), like bulls, like dogs (Psalm 22).

To those who live more securely, a preoccupation with enemies can seem paranoid. Yet we all have forces marshalled against us. St. Paul tells us that our struggle is with "the rulers...of this present darkness," and he urges, "Take up the whole armor of God" (Ephesians 6:12–13).

This is a psalm of embattled trustfulness, says Diane Bergant. The one in prayer sends out a distress signal.

Deliver me from evil, please,
inward and outward.

Be gracious to me, O God, for people trample on me;
all day long foes oppress me;
my enemies trample on me all day long,
for many fight against me.
O Most High, when I am afraid,
I put my trust in you.
In God, whose word I praise,
in God I trust; I am not afraid;
what can flesh do to me?
All day long they seek to injure my cause;
all their thoughts are against me for evil.
They stir up strife, they lurk,
they watch my steps.
As they hoped to have my life,
so repay them for their crime;
in wrath cast down the peoples, O God!
You have kept count of my tossings;
put my tears in your bottle.
Are they not in your record?
Then my enemies will retreat
in the day when I call.
This I know, that God is for me.
In God, whose word I praise,
in the LORD, whose word I praise,
in God I trust; I am not afraid.

Psalm 62

(vv. 1–9)

Psalm 62 begins with the soul, the vital force of the speaker, enjoying a kind of Sabbath rest. God is our ground of confidence. The next verse puts it even more strongly: God "alone is my rock and my salvation, / my fortress; I shall never be shaken." No metaphor in the Bible appears more often: God is my rock.

The landscape of Israel gave rise to this image. John McKenzie, SJ, in his *Dictionary of the Bible*, tells us "rock" is a divine title. "The title clearly suggests ancient warfare; if one could establish a position on one of the precipitous crags so numerous in Palestine, one could resist almost any attack." Machaerus was one such fortress rock, which took the besieging Romans a year to capture.

In trouble, we anchor ourselves solidly on the Lord, or we take refuge behind this bulwark. "Trust in [God] at all times, O people."

Dear God, my rock,
help me bear all the buffets.

40

For God alone my soul waits in silence;
from him comes my salvation.
He alone is my rock and my salvation,
my fortress; I shall never be shaken.
How long will you assail a person,
will you batter your victim, all of you,
as you would a leaning wall, a tottering fence?
Their only plan is to bring down a person of prominence.
They take pleasure in falsehood;
they bless with their mouths,
but inwardly they curse.
For God alone my soul waits in silence,
for my hope is from him.
He alone is my rock and my salvation,
my fortress; I shall not be shaken.
On God rests my deliverance and my honor;
my mighty rock, my refuge is in God.
Trust in him at all times, O people;
pour out your heart before him;
God is a refuge for us.

Psalm 84

(vv. 1–7, 10)

Psalm 84 starts out with a pure desire for God, for the house of God. "My soul longs, indeed it faints...My heart and my flesh sing for joy." In God's holy place the simplest creatures peacefully dwell: "the sparrow finds a home / and the swallow a nest..."

The desire to be equally blessed, to make one's home there in the sanctuary, provokes one to go on pilgrimage. Such a spiritual journey is not tiring but invigorating. "They go from strength to strength; / the God of gods will be seen in Zion."

Upon arrival at the sanctuary in the holy city, the pilgrim sings out in exultation: "A day in your courts is better / than a thousand elsewhere."

The divine presence is everywhere, but thanks be to those sites—churches, shrines, icons, inner rooms—which make us most at home with God.

I'm on the way to your dwelling,
and already in it!

How lovely is your dwelling place,
O LORD of hosts!
My soul longs, indeed it faints
for the courts of the LORD;
my heart and my flesh sing for joy
to the living God.
Even the sparrow finds a home,
and the swallow a nest for herself,
where she may lay her young,
at your altars, O LORD of hosts,
my King and my God.
Happy are those who live in your house,
ever singing your praise.
Happy are those whose strength is in you,
in whose heart are the highways to Zion.
As they go through the valley of Baca
they make it a place of springs;
the early rain also covers it with pools.
They go from strength to strength;
the God of gods will be seen in Zion.
For a day in your courts is better
than a thousand elsewhere.

Psalm 88

(vv. 1–5, 13–18)

A psalm, by definition, is for singing. But how can one possibly sing these desolate words? That can be asked of all the psalms of lament, but the rest of them come to a resolution, a closing note of hope and trust. Psalm 88 concludes on this note: "My companions are in darkness."

Several years ago, on my first visit to the Holy Land, we were taken to the house of Caiaphas. It has a dungeon, a dark pit hollowed out in the rock. Jesus is thought to have been confined there after his capture in the Garden. Our group descended to it. In the dark, by flashlight, someone read this psalm: "I am counted with those who go down to the Pit."

In Psalm 88, though we flinch from this outcry, we can glimpse what pushes many people to suicide and keeps others right on the brink. Jesus on the cross keenly felt the absence of God but still held strongly to the presence. His hand is out to anyone feeling so abandoned.

Help me resonate with those in the Pit,
and to be always trusting.

O LORD, God of my salvation,
when, at night, I cry out in your presence,
let my prayer come before you;
incline your ear to my cry.
For my soul is full of troubles,
and my life draws near to Sheol.
I am counted among those who go down to the Pit;
I am like those who have no help,
like those forsaken among the dead,
like the slain that lie in the grave,
But I, O LORD, cry out to you;
in the morning my prayer comes before you.
O LORD, why do you cast me off?
Why do you hide your face from me?
Wretched and close to death from my youth up,
I suffer your terrors; I am desperate.
Your wrath has swept over me;
your dread assaults destroy me.
They surround me like a flood all day long;
from all sides they close in on me.
You have caused friend and neighbor to shun me;
my companions are in darkness.

Your steadfast love, O LORD, extends to the heavens,

your faithfulness
   to the clouds.
Your righteousness is like
   the mighty mountains,
your judgments are like
   the great deep;
you save humans
   and animals alike,
      O LORD.

Psalm 36:5–6

Psalm 91

This is the psalm with which the devil tempts Jesus to impressive display, the sin of presumption—to cast himself down from the parapet of the Temple, counting on very special protection. The Deceiver twists the psalm so as to urge something rash, whereas it is really about resting secure in the Most High despite all threats.

In a tiny, precarious country, the Lord's protection is promised not only against armed invaders but just as surely against rampant disease and whatever troubles the spirit, both the noonday devil and "the terror of the night."

Imagery of the eagle reinforces this message, allusion to that great seven- or eight-foot span of wings thrown over its nestlings. And angels, adversaries of the demonic, assure divine protection to one who clings with faith.

Small wonder that Psalm 91 has continued as a beacon, a favorite resource, throughout the centuries.

With God our Providence,
how can I not be trusting?

You who live in the shelter of the Most High,
who abide in the shadow of the Almighty,
will say to the LORD, "My refuge and my fortress;
my God, in whom I trust."
For he will deliver you from the snare of the fowler
and from the deadly pestilence;
he will cover you with his pinions,
and under his wings you will find refuge;
his faithfulness is a shield and buckler.
You will not fear the terror of the night,
or the arrow that flies by day,
or the pestilence that stalks in darkness,
or the destruction that wastes at noonday.
A thousand may fall at your side,
ten thousand at your right hand,
but it will not come near you.
You will only look with your eyes
and see the punishment of the wicked.
Because you have made the LORD your refuge,
the Most High your dwelling place,
no evil shall befall you,
no scourge come near your tent.
For he will command his angels concerning you
to guard you in all your ways.
On their hands they will bear you up,
so that you will not dash your foot against a stone.

Psalm 100

What could be more transparent than Psalm 100? It is a profession of faith that the Lord YHWH is God, our creator and the shepherd of Israel. As members of God's people, we are drawn to his courts to join in praise. The psalm ends on its dominant note of thankfulness.

Our psalm has long been known as the Old Hundredth. It was translated in long meter (lines of 8 syllables, in four-line stanzas) for the *Geneva Psalter* in 1531, for communal singing of the psalms in the vernacular, as a mainspring of church life. Soon it was paraphrased by William Keith as the hymn, "All People that on Earth do Dwell," and its melody is well known.

All people that on earth do dwell,
Sing to the Lord with cheerful voice.
Him serve with fear, his praise forth tell,
Come ye before him and rejoice.

Sing out, my soul,
with all the music in me.

Make a joyful noise to the LORD, all the earth.
Worship the LORD with gladness;
come into his presence with singing.
Know that the LORD is God.
It is he that made us, and we are his;
we are his people, and the sheep of his pasture.
Enter his gates with thanksgiving,
and his courts with praise.
Give thanks to him, bless his name.
For the LORD is good;
his steadfast love endures forever,
and his faithfulness to all generations.

Psalm 103

(vv. 1–10)

We may consider Psalm 103 to be the peak of the psalter, so well is it structured, so memorable its images, and so welcome its theology of divine mercy.

The psalmist starts out by urging the *nepesh*, or life force, into thankfulness, into recognition that all is gift. To this person God has been redeemer from the Pit, the dark cavity that our sinfulness can plunge us into. We are brought back up into God's favor for a vigorous new start. "Your youth is renewed like the eagle's."

The whole of Psalm 103 comes to rest upon the following words: "The LORD is merciful and gracious, / slow to anger, and abounding in steadfast love." This is God's self-description on Mount Sinai, after letting Moses appeal for mercy (Exodus 34:6). This compact sentence runs as an undercurrent throughout the Bible, a corrective to images of a stern and harsh God. The present hymn, Psalm 103, is a prolonged meditation on this precious formula.

Merciful and gracious you still are,
my Lord.

Bless the LORD, O my soul,
and all that is within me,
bless his holy name.
Bless the LORD, O my soul,
and do not forget all his benefits—
who forgives all your iniquity,
who heals all your diseases,
who redeems your life from the Pit,
who crowns you with steadfast love and mercy,
who satisfies you with good as long as you live
so that your youth is renewed like the eagle's.
The LORD works vindication
and justice for all who are oppressed.
He made known his ways to Moses,
his acts to the people of Israel.
The LORD is merciful and gracious,
slow to anger and abounding in steadfast love.
He will not always accuse,
nor will he keep his anger forever.
He does not deal with us according to our sins,
nor repay us according to our iniquities.

Psalm 103

(vv. 11–18)

In the second movement of Psalm 103, "God's everlasting love is set side by side with human frailty" (*International Bible Commentary*). "As a father has compassion for his children, so the LORD has compassion for those who fear him." This sensitive God is not the father as disciplinarian, but the Creator who "knows how we were made…remembers that we are dust."

The psalm confesses the weakness of humankind, that our "days are like grass." Human evanescence serves here to highlight God's lasting mercy, which is "from everlasting to everlasting" and towers above our perishable state.

Salvation extends to the children's children of those who keep God's covenant. This assurance takes us back to Exodus and God's promise to continue in kindness for a thousand generations.

Psalm 103, after piling up reasons for gratitude, ends as it began: "Bless the LORD, O my soul!"

Fragile I truly am, and in need
of your bolstering.

For as the heavens are high above the earth,
so great is his steadfast love toward those who fear him;
as far as the east is from the west,
so far he removes our transgressions from us.
As a father has compassion for his children,
so the LORD has compassion for those who fear him.
For he knows how we were made;
he remembers that we are dust.
As for mortals, their days are like grass;
they flourish like a flower of the field;
for the wind passes over it, and it is gone,
and its place knows it no more.
But the steadfast love of the LORD
is from everlasting to everlasting
on those who fear him,
and his righteousness to children's children,
to those who keep his covenant
and remember to do his commandments.

Let the heavens be glad, and let the earth rejoice;

let the sea roar,
> and all that fills it;

let the field exult,
> and everything in it.

Then shall all the trees
> of the forest sing for joy

before the LORD;
> for he is coming,

for he is coming to judge
> the earth.

Psalm 96:11–13

Psalm 104

(vv. 1–9)

How is it that we find order and not chaos to be mostly the rule in the universe? Ancient people of the Near East, convinced that chaotic forces have a life of their own, sang of primordial warfare, with their deities prevailing. The first two verses of Genesis show God dispelling the universal dark and taming the uncontrollable waters, so as to construct upon them the huge disk of earth. Upper waters formed a dome, above which God made his palace.

We read in Psalm 104 of the Creator, who travels "on the wings of the wind" and is "wrapped in light as with a garment." It may well call up those images that Michelangelo left us on the roof of the Sistine Chapel.

The drama of God rebuking the flood waters leads into a section of the psalm depicting a well-watered and fertile earth. "The trees of the LORD are watered abundantly," and the birds nest there to sing. At night "young lions roar for their prey"; by day people go out to labor until evening falls. Our planet is in equilibrium.

> *Creator God,*
> *I am awe-struck.*

Bless the LORD, O my soul.
O LORD my God, you are very great.
You are clothed with honor and majesty,
wrapped in light as with a garment.
You stretch out the heavens like a tent,
you set the beams of your chambers on the waters,
you make the clouds your chariot,
you ride on the wings of the wind,
you make the winds your messengers,
fire and flame your ministers.
You set the earth on its foundations,
so that it shall never be shaken.
You cover it with the deep as with a garment;
the waters stood above the mountains.
At your rebuke they flee;
at the sound of your thunder they take to flight.
They rose up to the mountains, ran down to the valleys
to the place that you appointed for them.
You set a boundary that they may not pass,
so that they might not again cover the earth.

Psalm 104

(vv. 24–31)

Psalm 104, fairly long, ends with an exclamatory section expressive of wonder: "O LORD, how manifold are your works! / In wisdom you have made them all." The mighty sea, no longer ungovernable, teems with "innumerable" beings, "living things both small and great." The largest is Leviathan, no longer a Moby Dick of wickedness but a disporting creature formed by God to play with.

God is provider for all living things, which must recognize how dependent they are, beggars with outstretched hands. "Take away their breath, they die / and return to their dust." The breath of life, the *ruah* or spirit we all have, is the breath of God, and it goes back to God at death.

To counter mortality, the Creator gives life untiringly, and the church keeps praying: "Send forth your spirit, they are created / and you renew the face" of the earth.

Spirit of God,
breathe into me.

O LORD, how manifold are your works!
In wisdom you have made them all;
the earth is full of your creatures.
Yonder is the sea, great and wide,
creeping things innumerable are there,
living things both small and great.
There go the ships,
and Leviathan that you formed to sport in it.
These all look to you
to give them their food in due season;
when you give to them, they gather it up;
when you open your hand, they are filled with good things.
When you hide your face, they are dismayed;
when you take away their breath, they die
and return to their dust.
When you send forth your spirit, they are created;
and you renew the face of the ground.
May the glory of the LORD endure forever;
may the LORD rejoice in his works...

Psalm 110

Psalm 110 is historic, about David, the kingly regent of the Lord Yahweh. The scenario is of a royal enthronement and includes a promise of victory over malicious forces. In the received Christian reading, this psalm is held to prophesy Jesus, son of David, who will institute the kingdom of God.

There is a shock of violence in this psalm. As Richard Clifford explains, "The king's battles are the Lord's; such is the ideology of holy war...The king is charged with furthering divine justice in the world which, in biblical terms, means putting down the wicked and raising up the aggrieved innocent."

I read this psalm with a sort of split vision, looking to the Davidic king, who crushes enemies of the Chosen People, without losing sight of the promised Messiah. The nub of Psalm 110 is God's oath, "You are a priest forever according to the order of Melchizedeck," the priest-king of Genesis 14. The Letter to the Hebrews understands him as a figure of the priest-messiah.

Grant me dominion
over threats and enemies.

The LORD says to my lord,
"Sit at my right hand
until I make your enemies your footstool."
The LORD sends out from Zion
your mighty scepter.
Rule in the midst of your foes.
Your people will offer themselves willingly
on the day you lead your forces
on the holy mountains.
From the womb of the morning,
like dew, your youth will come to you.
The LORD has sworn and will not change his mind,
"You are a priest forever according to the order of
Melchizedek."
The Lord is at your right hand;
he will shatter kings on the day of his wrath.
He will execute judgment among the nations,
filling them with corpses;
he will shatter heads
over the wide earth.
He will drink from the stream by the path;
therefore he will lift up his head.

The righteous flourish like the palm tree,

and grow like a cedar
   in Lebanon.
They are planted
   in the house of the LORD;
they flourish in the courts
   of our God.
In old age they still
   produce fruit;
they are always green
   and full of sap.

Psalm 92:12–14

Psalm 111

In the Hebrew original, Psalm 111 is an acrostic psalm. Verse 1 begins with "A" (Aleph), verse 2 with "B" (Beth), and so on for the 22-letter alphabet. The opening word, "Hallelujah"—*hallelu* + *Jah*, praise Yahweh—attunes us to God's great works, God's "wonderful deeds" for the people. Among them is "the heritage of the nations": occupation of Canaan.

The Creator nourishes everyone on the earth, but in a special way "those who fear him." Biblically, to fear God does not mean cowering; it means awe and wonder at the supreme greatness and moral authority of God.

"The fear of the LORD is the beginning of wisdom." To revere the Omnipotent, the Father, is the start of a journey to absorption in divine love. In the Bible these two concepts, fear and love, often go hand in hand. Thanks to Isaiah (11:2), fear of the Lord was taken up in the church as among the seven gifts of the Holy Spirit.

Savior whom I revere,
turn my fearfulness into love.

Praise the LORD!
I will give thanks to the LORD with my whole heart,
in the company of the upright, in the congregation.
Great are the works of the LORD,
studied by all who delight in them.
Full of honor and majesty is his work,
and his righteousness endures forever.
He has gained renown by his wonderful deeds;
the LORD is gracious and merciful.
He provides food for those who fear him;
he is ever mindful of his covenant.
He has shown his people the power of his works,
in giving them the heritage of the nations.
The works of his hands are faithful and just;
all his precepts are trustworthy.
They are established forever and ever,
to be performed with faithfulness and uprightness.
He sent redemption to his people;
he has commanded his covenant forever.
Holy and awesome is his name.
The fear of the LORD is the beginning of wisdom;
all those who practice it have a good understanding.
His praise endures forever.

Psalm 114

Psalm 114 sums up in a pithy way the escape of the Chosen People from Egypt to their sacred land. Other psalms treat this forty-year epic at some length, telling its episodes. But Psalm 114 gives the history an imaginative twist. It views nature as responding with animation to the divine rescue.

The sea, a threatening force, has removed itself from the progress of the Jews like a panicky soldier before one mightier. The River Jordan also recoils. Since these waters are personified, the psalmist can taunt them, "Why is it, O sea, that you flee? / O Jordan, that you turn back?"

The mountains and hills, skipping like lambs, seem joyful and excited at the passage of God's people. The inanimate world thus proclaims the mastery of the Lord.

We can take Psalm 114 literally as tracing the flight of Israel from Egypt; as allegory, it speaks of our redemption wrought by Christ; the moral application is to conversion from sin to grace; finally, we leave human corruption for liberty in God's glory. How rich this psalm can be!

I want to stride ahead
into God's mystery.

PSALM 114

When Israel went out from Egypt,
the house of Jacob from a people of strange language,
Judah became God's sanctuary,
Israel his dominion.
The sea looked and fled;
Jordan turned back.
The mountains skipped like rams,
the hills like lambs.
Why is it, O sea, that you flee?
O Jordan, that you turn back?
O mountains, that you skip like rams?
O hills, like lambs?
Tremble, O earth, at the presence of the LORD,
at the presence of the God of Jacob,
who turns the rock into a pool of water,
the flint into a spring of water.

Psalm 116

(vv. 1–2, 12–15, 18–19)

The speaker of this psalm is asking earnestly, "What shall I return to the LORD / for all his bounty to me?" Before the liturgical changes of Vatican Council II, the priest used to say these words to himself in Latin just before receiving the Body of Christ. He answered his own question: "I will lift up the cup of salvation, and call on the name of the LORD."

A toast is being raised. The "cup" in Bible parlance stands for something to be partaken in full measure. For Jesus it was the cup of bitterness, which became our cup of remedy.

Anyone who has made earnest promises to the Lord — marriage vows, ordination promises, religious profession — can chime in with these words of Psalm 116: "I will pay my vows to the LORD / in the presence of all his people."

Help me live out
my promises unstintingly.

PSALM 116:1–2, 12–15, 18–19

I love the LORD, because he has heard
my voice and my supplications.
Because he inclined his ear to me,
therefore I will call on him as long as I live....
What shall I return to the LORD
for all his bounty to me?
I will lift up the cup of salvation
and call on the name of the LORD,
I will pay my vows to the LORD
in the presence of all his people.
Precious in the sight of the LORD
is the death of his faithful ones....
I will pay my vows to the LORD
in the presence of all his people,
in the courts of the house of the LORD,
in your midst, O Jerusalem.
Praise the LORD!

Psalm 118

In Psalm 118, after a brief litany of praise, the psalmist recounts the hostility of surrounding peoples ("They surrounded me like bees"), and he exults over God's help in crushing them.

This latter part of the psalm is described by Dianne Bergant as "a liturgical celebration of thanks." When we hear "Open to me the gates of righteousness," we are to think of the entrance to the Jerusalem temple. Reading the psalm in terms of our own spiritual reality, we plead for admission into God's holiness and to be kept there.

"The stone that the builders rejected has become the chief cornerstone," is a proverb, we are told. Who or what is the stone? The early church had no doubt, since Jesus applied the words to himself.

The day of victory over evil is surely a "day that the LORD has made." In the Christian view this can only be Easter, the day of the resurrection of the Messiah, "the one who comes." So much reason we have to "rejoice and be glad!"

Draw me into your holiness,
dear Lord.

Open to me the gates of righteousness,
that I may enter through them
and give thanks to the LORD.
This is the gate of the LORD;
the righteous shall enter through it.
I thank you that you have answered me
and have become my salvation.
The stone that the builders rejected
has become the chief cornerstone.
This is the LORD's doing;
it is marvelous in our eyes.
This is the day that the LORD has made;
let us rejoice and be glad in it.
Save us, we beseech you, O LORD!
O LORD, we beseech you, give us success!
Blessed is the one who comes in the name of the LORD.
We bless you from the house of the LORD.
The LORD is God,
and he has given us light.
Bind the festal procession with branches,
up to the horns of the altar.

John Griesbach

I know all the birds of the air,

and all that moves

in the field is mine.

Psalm 50:11

Psalm 119

(vv. 97–105)

Verse 1 sets the theme of all 176 verses of Psalm 119: "Happy those whose way is blameless, who walk in the law of the LORD." Endless variations follow, chant-like.

Psalm 119 is composed with frontal rhyme (rhyme at the start of lines) in packets of eight verses, each verse opening with the same letter of the Hebrew alphabet. Translations cannot duplicate this rhyme. The psalm thus includes twenty-two packets. Here we have the letter "Mem," followed by the opening verse of the next letter, "Nun."

Psalm 119, far from an exercise in artistic cleverness, is an evocation of Wisdom, a prolonged attention to Torah, divine teaching. Almost every verse mentions *torah* or one of its synonyms—judgment, testimony, precept, promise, way, command, and, of course, law. The prevailing tone, as Diane Bergant points out, is the "attitude of docility," a readiness to be taught by the Lord.

In our feisty selection, the psalmist enthuses about how he loves the law.

> *Alas, dear God, what a wavery student*
> *I am of your will.*

[Mem]
Oh, how I love your law!
It is my meditation all day long.
Your commandment makes me wiser than my enemies,
for it is always with me.
I have more understanding than all my teachers,
for your decrees are my meditation.
I understand more than the aged,
for I keep your precepts.
I hold back my feet from every evil way,
in order to keep your word.
I do not turn away from your ordinances,
for you have taught me.
How sweet are your words to my taste,
sweeter than honey to my mouth!
Through your precepts I get understanding;
therefore I hate every false way.

[Nun]
Your word is a lamp to my feet
and a light to my path.

Psalm 121

Blessed is anyone who lives within sight of mountains (or "hills," in this translation). They lift up the spirit. I think of the artist Paul Cézanne, forever painting Mont St. Victoire, near his home. By solidity and majesty and height, mountains suggest divinity.

Scholars interpret this as a pilgrimage hymn. In the psalter it is called "a Song of Ascents." The journey to Jerusalem from anywhere in Israel was an ascent—with hazards—to the Holy City and the heights around it.

The word that leaps out from the poem as its motif is "keeper," meaning "guard" or "guardian." "He who keeps Israel / will never slumber nor sleep."

This is such a trustful psalm. It gives us one of those reliable mantras: "My help comes from the LORD, / who made heaven and earth." Psalm 121 is well worth knowing by heart. When backed up in traffic or in lines, recite it!

My Keeper, in all extremities
may I turn to you.

PSALM 121

I lift up my eyes to the hills—
from where will my help come?
My help comes from the LORD,
who made heaven and earth.
He will not let your foot be moved;
he who keeps you will not slumber.
He who keeps Israel
will neither slumber nor sleep.
The LORD is your keeper;
the LORD is your shade at your right hand.
The sun shall not strike you by day,
nor the moon by night.
The LORD will keep you from all evil;
he will keep your life.
The LORD will keep
your going out and your coming in
from this time on and forevermore.

Psalm 122

People still feel excitement when embarking on pilgrimage—to Lourdes or Guadalupe or Jerusalem. And how overwhelmed they feel once they are standing there.

The Museum of Israel, in Jerusalem, has a scale model of the old walled city that Jesus visited. It was indeed compact. The Temple, "the house of the LORD," was the pilgrims' true objective; but their feeling of awe and happiness attached to the city, where judgment was rendered and the twelve disparate tribes intermingled.

The psalm seems to conclude back home. The pilgrim, full of the experience, exclaims in benediction: "Peace be within you!" Anyone arriving today to visit Calvary and the Holy Sepulcher will breathe the same petition.

"O what a beautiful city!" Marian Anderson sang, in her 1942 concert at the Lincoln Memorial, echoing the close of the Book of Revelation. That is what we hear in Psalm 122.

Give me longing for your city
and energy to contribute.

PSALM 122

I was glad when they said to me,
"Let us go to the house of the LORD!"
Our feet are standing
within your gates, O Jerusalem.
Jerusalem—built as a city
that is bound firmly together.
To it the tribes go up,
the tribes of the LORD,
as was decreed for Israel,
to give thanks to the name of the LORD.
For there the thrones for judgment were set up,
the thrones of the house of David.
Pray for the peace of Jerusalem:
"May they prosper who love you.
Peace be within your walls,
and security within your towers."
For the sake of my relatives and friends
I will say, "Peace be within you."
For the sake of the house of the LORD our God,
I will seek your good.

Psalm 126

Psalm 126, one of the Songs of Ascents, begins on a jubilant note. A communal voice speaks of the reversal of fortune when the Persian emperor Cyrus, taking over Babylon, was inspired to send home the enslaved Jews. "When the LORD restored the fortunes of Zion, / we were like those who dream." What a reprieve!

The psalm takes a mystifying turn to pray for a restoration of captives, as if the promise had only been dreamed of but not yet realized. "Restore our fortunes, O LORD," it says, just as you fill up the dry streams of the Negeb in flash floods.

A proverb, a wisdom saying, then serves to unite the apparent contraries: "Those who sow in tears / reap with shouts of joy." How spiritually suggestive this is. Trials and illness and dark nights are a sure path to fruitfulness. Hard farm work of the spirit leads to a harvest, as we hear in the gospel song "Bringing in the Sheaves."

Please, Lord, may our valley of tears
be fruitful.

When the LORD restored the fortunes of Zion,
we were like those who dream.
Then our mouth was filled with laughter,
and our tongue with shouts of joy;
then it was said among the nations,
"The LORD has done great things for them."
The LORD has done great things for us,
and we rejoiced.
Restore our fortunes, O LORD,
like the watercourses in the Negeb.
May those who sow in tears
reap with shouts of joy.
Those who go out weeping,
bearing the seed for sowing,
shall come home with shouts of joy,
carrying their sheaves.

Let the floods clap their hands;

let the hills sing together
for joy
at the presence of the LORD,
for he is coming
to judge the earth.

Psalm 98:8–9

Psalm 130

This psalm, known in Latin by its opening words, *De Profundis*, "out of the depths," is numbered by the church among the seven penitential psalms. It begins at an extreme of guilt or desperation, as when King David was faced with his sins, or when Queen Esther cried out for divine help against the extinction of her people.

One does not need to have hit bottom to utter this prayer. Some self-awareness can remind us that we are indeed dust and ashes, as Ash Wednesday insists. Even so, we can make our abject state into an appeal for clemency, as the psalmist does in strangely calming words: "If you, O LORD, should mark iniquities, / Lord, who could stand?"

This prayer can induce us to hopeful waiting, like a watchman anxious to see the dawn. How striking it is that in Spanish the verb "to wait" is the same word as "to hope": *esperar*.

Lord, keep me on the lookout
for your mercies.

Out of the depths I cry to you, O LORD.
Lord, hear my voice!
Let your ears be attentive
to the voice of my supplications!
If you, O LORD, should mark iniquities,
Lord, who could stand?
But there is forgiveness with you,
so that you may be revered.
I wait for the LORD, my soul waits,
and in his word I hope;
my soul waits for the Lord
more than those who watch for the morning,
more than those who watch for the morning.
O Israel, hope in the LORD!
For with the LORD there is steadfast love,
and with him is great power to redeem.
It is he who will redeem Israel
from all its iniquities.

Psalm 139

Some Mexican homes display a small triangle with an eye in the middle, *el Ojo de Dios*, the eye of God. Omniscience, omnipotence, omnipresence—the psalmist imagines how these great attributes of God are impacting him. God takes such an inquiring interest—probing (as if poking!), checking one's motives, tracking one's steps. How fully God registers us!

The psalm even has a horror-movie touch: "You hem me in, behind and before / and lay your hand upon me." We have an impulse to flee; yet who can outrun God? Even in flight, this very hand that formed and knitted us would guide and uphold us.

And so Psalm 139 moves us from fear to appreciation. The psalmist grows from insecure teenager to grateful believer in God's all-positive, all-creative love. "I praise you, for I am fearfully and wonderfully made. / Wonderful are your works!"

In awe and trembling,
I begin to take heart.

PSALM 139:1, 5–14

O Lord, you have searched me and known me.
You know when I sit down and when I rise up...
You hem me in, behind and before,
and lay your hand upon me.
Such knowledge is too wonderful for me;
it is so high that I cannot attain it.
Where can I go from your spirit?
Or where can I flee from your presence?
If I ascend to heaven, you are there;
if I make my bed in Sheol, you are there.
If I take the wings of the morning
and settle at the farthest limits of the sea,
even there your hand shall lead me,
and your right hand shall hold me fast.
If I say, "Surely the darkness shall cover me,
and the light around me become night,"
even the darkness is not dark to you;
the night is as bright as the day,
for darkness is as light to you.

For it was you who formed my inward parts;
you knit me together in my mother's womb.
I praise you, for I am fearfully and wonderfully made.
Wonderful are your works;
that I know very well.

Psalm 150

Psalm 150 is a liturgy of praises sung out in the holy place, God's sanctuary. The Lord is being lauded for "mighty deeds" and "surpassing greatness." For the Jews, "mighty deeds" is shorthand for the rescue from Egypt and delivery from the exile in Babylon. "Surpassing greatness" expresses the kingship of a Creator still forming our earth through the vast forces that keep us feeling so small.

God's works, celebrated in 150 psalms, deserve the solemnity of this finale, which is so musical. We get an inventory of the instruments in play long before Jesus, the loud ones—cymbals crashing and horns resounding—plus the quietest, such as the lute and the harp. All of these harmonics set the worshipers dancing.

"Let everything that breathes praise the Lord." In a universe full of the incomprehensible and the violent, we still believe in a great goodness steering us. "Alleluia!"

> *My entire being,*
> *be a continual hymn.*

PSALM 150

Praise the LORD!
Praise God in his sanctuary;
praise him in his mighty firmament!
Praise him for his mighty deeds;
praise him according to his surpassing greatness!
Praise him with trumpet sound;
praise him with lute and harp!
Praise him with tambourine and dance;
praise him with strings and pipe!
Praise him with clanging cymbals;
praise him with loud clashing cymbals!
Let everything that breathes praise the LORD!
Praise the LORD!

Steadfast love and faithfulness will meet;

righteousness and peace
will kiss each other.
Faithfulness will spring up
from the ground,
and righteousness will look
down from the sky.
The LORD will give what
is good,
and our land will yield
its increase.

Psalm 85:10–12